# Neptune

by Gregory L. Vogt

Consultant:
Ralph Winrich
Aerospace Education Specialist
for NASA

Bridgestone Books
an imprint of Capstone Press
Mankato, Minnesota

Bridgestone Books are published by Capstone Press
151 Good Counsel Drive, P.O. Box 669, Mankato, Minnesota 56002
http://www.capstone-press.com

*Library of Congress Cataloging-in-Publication Data*
Vogt, Gregory.
     Neptune/by Gregory L. Vogt.
        p. cm.—(The galaxy)
     Includes bibliographical references and index.
     Summary: Discusses the orbit, atmosphere, moons, surface features, exploration, and
other aspects of the planet Neptune.
     ISBN 0-7368-0513-3
     1. Neptune (Planet)—Juvenile literature. [1. Neptune (Planet)] I. Title. II. Series.
QB691 .V643  2000
523.48′1—dc21                                                                                    99-086979

**Editorial Credits**
Erika Mikkelson, editor; Timothy Halldin, cover designer and illustrator;
     Kimberly Danger and Jodi Theisen, photo researchers

**Photo Credits**
Astronomical Society of the Pacific/NASA, 6, 10, 12, 18, 20
NASA, cover, 1, 8, 14, 16

1 2 3 4 5 6 05 04 03 02 01 00

# Table of Contents

# Relative size of the Sun and the planets

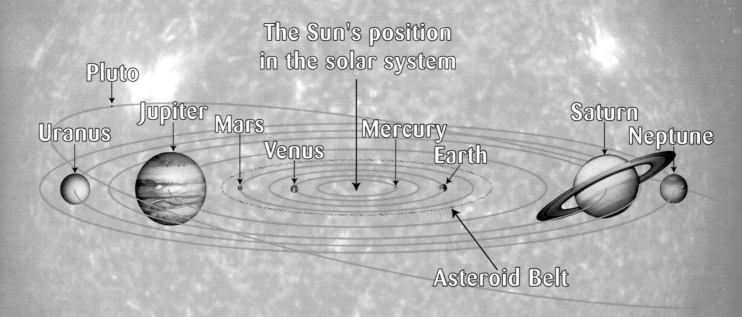

The Sun's position
in the solar system

Pluto

Uranus

Jupiter

Mars

Venus

Mercury

Earth

Saturn

Neptune

Asteroid Belt

**The Sun**

Neptune is one of nine planets in the solar system. The Sun is the center of the solar system. Planets, asteroids, and comets travel around the Sun.

Mercury, Venus, Earth, and Mars are the closest planets to the Sun. These inner planets are made of rock. Jupiter, Saturn, Uranus, and Neptune are the outer planets. These giant planets are made of gases. Pluto is the farthest planet from the Sun. Pluto is made of rock and ice.

Neptune is the eighth planet from the Sun. It is the fourth largest of the nine planets in the solar system. Neptune is visible from Earth with binoculars or a small telescope.

This illustration compares the sizes of the planets and the Sun. Neptune is the fourth largest planet. The blue lines show the orbits of the planets. Thousands of asteroids move around the Sun. The asteroid belt is between the orbits of Mars and Jupiter.

# FAST FACTS

|  | Neptune | Earth |
|---|---|---|
| **Diameter:** | 30,776 miles (49,530 kilometers) | 7,927 miles (12,756 kilometers) |
| **Average distance from the Sun:** | 2,797 million miles (4,501 million kilometers) | 93 million miles (150 million kilometers) |
| **Revolution period:** | 165 years | 365 days, 6 hours |
| **Rotation period:** | 16 hours, 17 minutes | 23 hours, 56 minutes |
| **Moons:** | 8 | 1 |

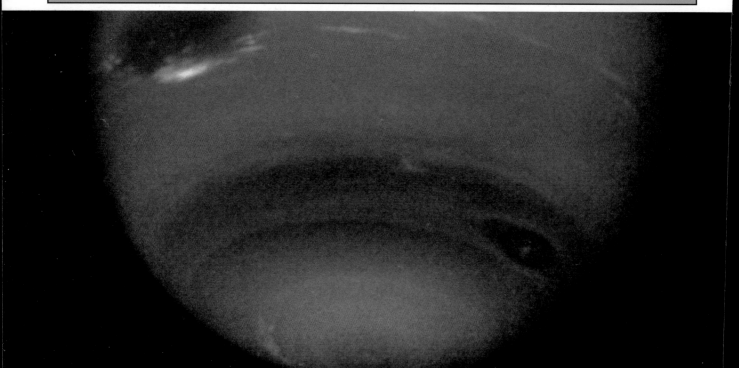

# The Planet Neptune

In 1846, French mathematician Urbain Leverrier and Englishman John Couch Adams searched for an undiscovered planet. They thought a planet was affecting the motion of Uranus. Leverrier wrote to Johann Galle at the Berlin Observatory in Germany. He told Galle to point his telescope to a certain part of the sky. Galle discovered Neptune the same day he read Leverrier's letter.

Neptune is one of the giant planets. Neptune is 30,776 miles (49,530 kilometers) wide. Sixty planets the size of Earth could fit inside Neptune.

Neptune is one of the coldest planets in the solar system. The temperature is about minus 360 degrees Fahrenheit (minus 218 degrees Celsius) on the planet's surface.

**The methane in Neptune's atmosphere gives the planet its blue color.**

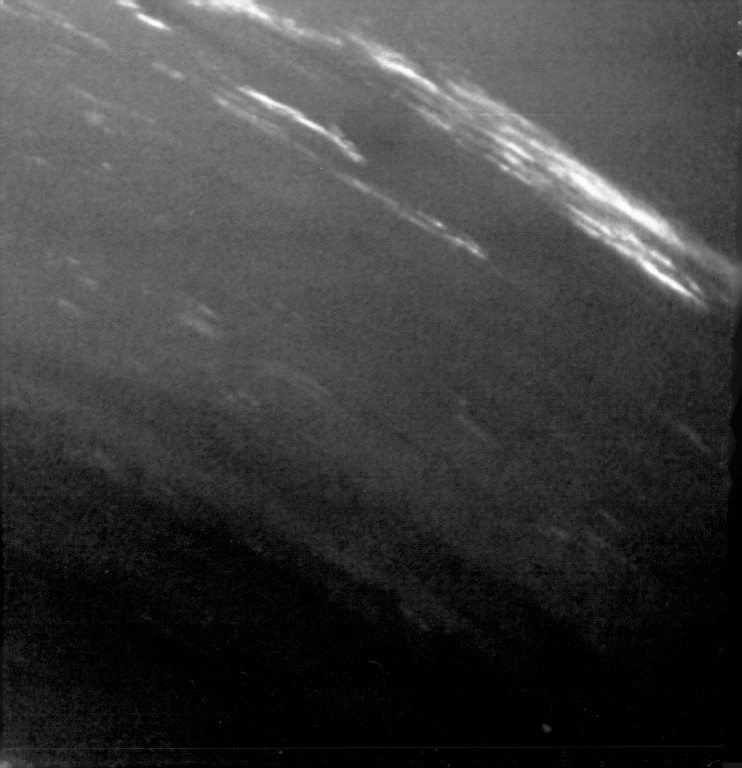

# Atmosphere

Neptune is mainly made of hydrogen, helium, and methane gases. These gases make up the atmosphere that surrounds Neptune. Methane gives Neptune its blue color.

Light-colored bands of clouds circle Neptune. Winds that often reach 1,500 miles (2,400 kilometers) per hour blow the clouds. Neptune has stronger winds than any other planet. Astronomers named one cloud Scooter because it scoots quickly around Neptune.

Storms appear in Neptune's atmosphere as large spots. One famous spot is no longer visible today. The Great Dark Spot was a giant storm that formed in Neptune's atmosphere. The storm was as big as Earth. The *Voyager 2* space probe photographed the storm in 1989. In 1994, the Hubble Space Telescope photographed Neptune. The Great Dark Spot had disappeared from Neptune's atmosphere.

**Strong winds blow the clouds in Neptune's atmosphere.**

# Rings

In 1981, astronomers watched Neptune pass directly in front of a star. The star blinked off and on four times just before Neptune passed in front of the star. The star blinked off and on again just after the planet passed it. The blinking of the star meant that Neptune had four rings circling it.

Astronomers were not sure if Neptune's rings were full circles. The rings looked like they were missing long chunks. Astronomers called the rings ring arcs.

Scientists saw photographs of the rings when *Voyager 2* passed Neptune in 1989. The parts of the rings that appeared to be missing were there. Those areas of the rings were made of dark dust and could not be seen from Earth.

Astronomers named the four rings. The ring closest to Neptune is Diffuse. Astronomers call the next ring Inner. The third ring is called Plateau. Main is the farthest ring from Neptune.

**Neptune's rings are made of small, dust-like particles.**

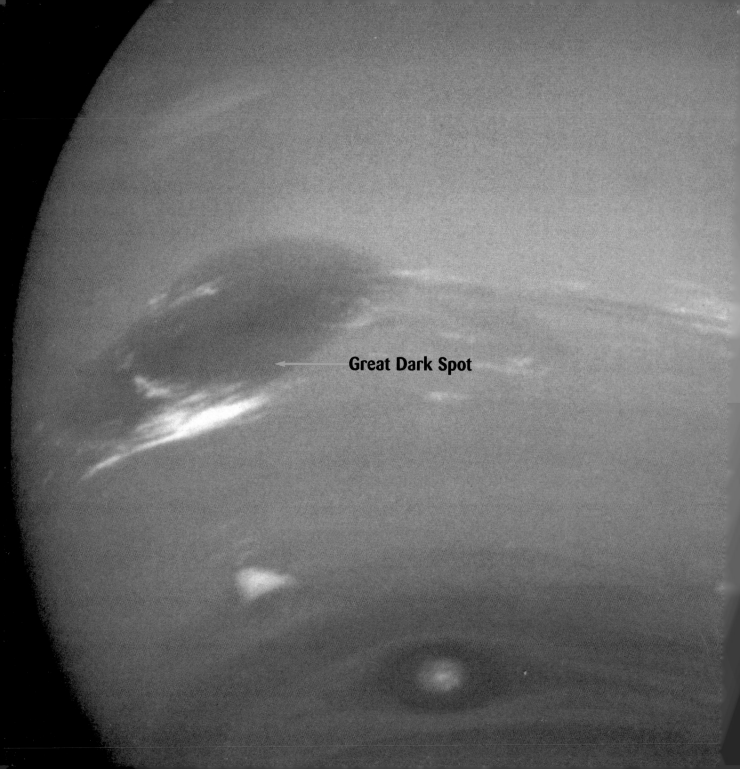
Great Dark Spot

Neptune makes one revolution around the Sun every 165 years. The planet travels slowly. Every second, Neptune moves almost 3.5 miles (6 kilometers) in its orbit. In the same time, Earth travels 18.5 miles (30 kilometers).

Neptune usually is the eighth planet in distance from the Sun. But Pluto sometimes dips inside Neptune's orbit. At these times, Neptune is the farthest planet from the Sun.

Neptune rotates as it orbits. The planet spins once every 16 hours and 7 minutes. The direction of the spin is tilted on an axis. Neptune spins around this imaginary line running through its center.

Because Neptune is tilted, the planet has summer and winter seasons that each last 40 years. During the summer, Neptune's axis tilts toward the Sun. The planet's axis tilts away from the Sun during the winter.

**Scientists learned about Neptune's rotation by watching the Great Dark Spot. Each time it came into view, they knew that Neptune had made one rotation.**

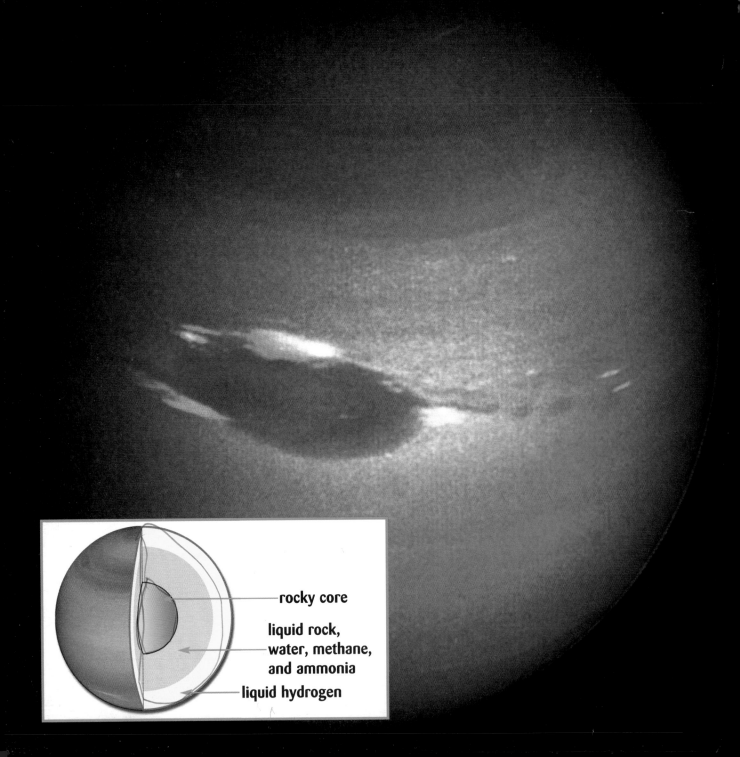

rocky core

liquid rock, water, methane, and ammonia

liquid hydrogen

# Inside Neptune

Scientists believe Neptune has four layers. Neptune's center is rock. A layer of liquid rock, water, methane, and ammonia surround Neptune's center. Farther from the center is a layer of liquid hydrogen. The atmosphere makes up the outer layer of Neptune.

Methane particles on Neptune are always changing. Heat from the Sun breaks down the methane in Neptune's upper atmosphere. The methane particles sink. The particles become colder and freeze into ice as they drop through the atmosphere. This process is called condensation.

The ice particles soon reach a warmer layer of the atmosphere. They melt together to become liquid methane. The methane then rises to the top of the atmosphere. This process is called evaporation. The process starts all over again when the methane gas rises to the top of Neptune's atmosphere.

**Condensation and evaporation change the methane gases in Neptune's atmosphere.**

This symbol represents Neptune. All planets except Earth are named for characters in Greek or Roman myths. In these ancient stories, Neptune was the Roman god of the sea.

## Moons

Eight moons orbit Neptune. The largest moon is Triton. This moon is 1,678 miles (2,700 kilometers) wide. The smallest moon is Naiad. It is 36 miles (58 kilometers) wide. Astronomers knew about only three moons before *Voyager 2* passed Neptune. They discovered five additional moons with pictures from *Voyager 2*.

Astronomers named Neptune's eight moons. Naiad and Thalassa are the closest moons to Neptune. The next four moons are Despina, Galatea, Larissa, and Proteus. Triton is the seventh moon from Neptune. Nereid is the farthest moon from Neptune.

Astronomers have learned a great deal about Triton. But they know very little about Neptune's other moons. Astronomers know that Naiad, Thalassa, Despina, and Galatea are dark moons. Astronomers also know the size of each moon. But they do not know what makes up the moons.

**This image shows the edges of Neptune and Triton.**

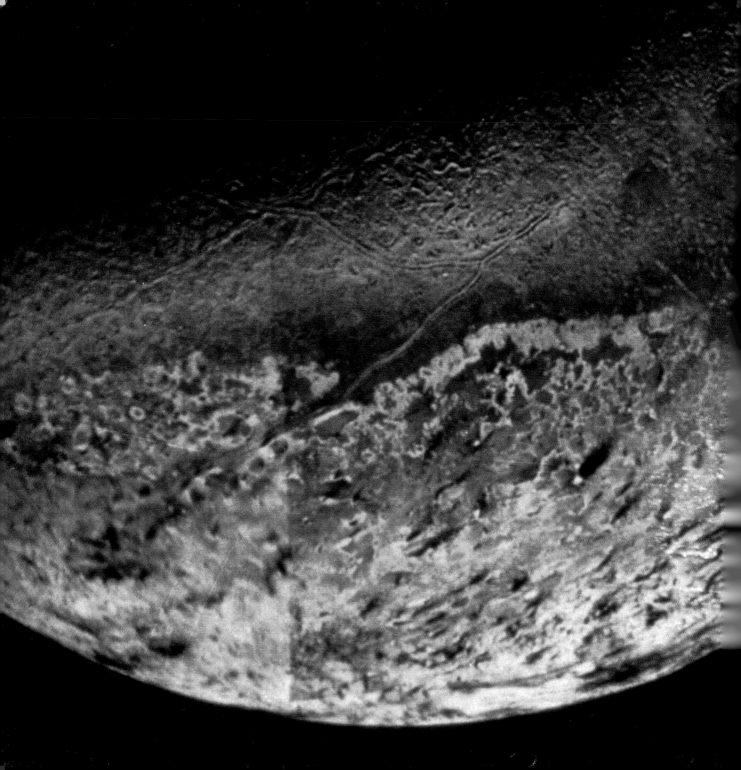

Astronomers have studied Triton. This moon is different from Neptune's seven other moons. Triton is lighter in color. An ice cap of frozen methane and nitrogen covers part of Triton. Other areas of Triton have many craters made by meteorite strikes.

Triton has a thin atmosphere. Some of Triton's atmosphere comes from geysers on the planet's surface. These holes spray out nitrogen and dust. The gas and dust travel far above the moon's surface.

Triton orbits Neptune in the opposite direction of the planet's other moons. Scientists think Triton used to orbit the Sun. A long time ago, Triton probably passed near Neptune. The planet's gravity captured the moon.

Triton is slowly moving closer to Neptune. The moon will travel too close to Neptune in about 10 million to 100 million years. Neptune's gravity will rip the moon apart. The pieces probably will become another ring around the planet.

**Geysers on Triton's surface produce nitrogen and dust.**

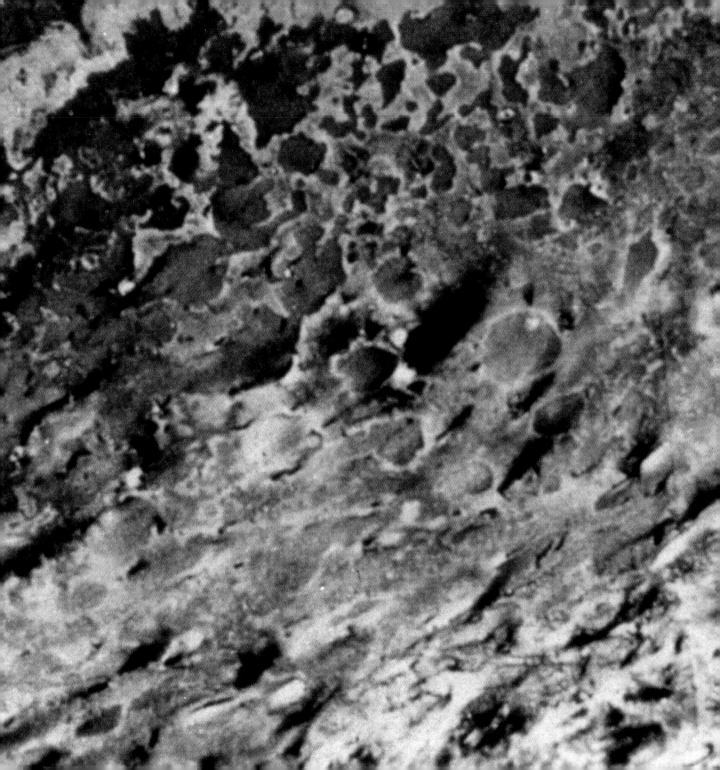

# Exploring Neptune

Neptune is difficult to see without binoculars or a telescope. The Hubble Space Telescope orbits Earth and takes pictures of Neptune. But the best pictures of Neptune and Triton came from the *Voyager 2* space probe.

*Voyager 2* explored many planets in the solar system. The space probe passed Jupiter, Saturn, and Uranus before reaching Neptune. *Voyager 2* took 9,000 pictures of Neptune, its rings, and its moons. Astronomers compare these pictures with pictures from the Hubble Space Telescope. Comparing the pictures can show how the planet changes over time.

Scientists continue to receive data about objects in the solar system from *Voyager 2*. Scientists believe the instruments on *Voyager 2* will keep working until about 2010. By then, the power will be too low for the instruments to work.

*Voyager 2* sent this close-up image of Triton's surface to scientists on Earth.

# Hands On: Evaporation

Evaporation occurs in Neptune's atmosphere. This change causes the liquid methane to turn into a gas. Evaporation occurs on Earth as well. You can see how evaporation changes a water into a gas.

## What You Need

A clear plastic container
Measuring cup
Water
Permanent marker

Ruler
A piece of paper
Pen or pencil

## What You Do

1. Use the measuring cup to put 2 cups (500 milliliters) of water into the container.
2. Use the marker to mark the water line on the container. Use the ruler to measure how high the water is. Write this number on a piece of paper.
3. Check the container every day for a week. Use the ruler to measure the water level.
4. Write down the measurements you take each day. How much water evaporated in a week?

Evaporation causes the water to turn into a gas called water vapor. You cannot see the water once it has become water vapor.